American Moments

ABDO & Daughters

SPIRIT OF ST. LOUIS

Rachel A. Koestler-Grack

VISIT US AT
WWW.ABDOPUB.COM

Published by ABDO Publishing Company, 4940 Viking Drive, Suite 622, Edina, Minnesota 55435. Copyright © 2005 by Abdo Consulting Group, Inc. International copyrights reserved in all countries. No part of this book may be reproduced in any form without written permission from the publisher. ABDO & Daughters™ is a trademark and logo of ABDO Publishing Company.

Printed in the United States.

Edited by: Melanie A. Howard
Interior Production and Design: Terry Dunham Incorporated
Cover Design: Mighty Media
Photos: Corbis; Library of Congress; Lindbergh Picture Collection.
        Manuscripts and Archives, Yale University

Library of Congress Cataloging-in-Publication Data

Koestler-Grack, Rachel A., 1973-
    Spirit of St. Louis / Rachel A. Koestler-Grack.
      p. cm. -- (American moments)
    Includes index.
    ISBN 1-59197-940-4
     1. Lindbergh, Charles A. (Charles Augustus), 1902-1974--Juvenile literature.
    2. Air pilots--United States--Biography--Juvenile literature.
    3. Transatlantic flights--Juvenile literature. 4. Spirit of St. Louis (Airplane)--Juvenile
    literature. I. Title. II. Series.

TL540.L5K64 2005
629.13'092--dc22
                                                        2004066017

CONTENTS

ALONE OVER THE ATLANTIC

Charles Lindbergh had been flying for 14 hours over the Atlantic Ocean in a single-engine plane. He had left from New York City, New York, just before 8:00 AM Eastern Standard Time on the morning of May 20, 1927. Now it was night. The only light came from the eerie green glow of his instrument panel. He was cold and tired.

Lindbergh's fate relied on his flying instruments. He carefully monitored every fluctuation the needles of his gauges made. Suddenly, he remembered there was more to consider outside the cockpit. He grabbed his flashlight and stuck his arm out the window. The surface of the engine looked shiny in the beam of light. *Ice!* Lindbergh thought.

If ice built up on the plane, his instruments might fail. Lindbergh and his plane, the *Spirit of St. Louis*, would plunge into the chilling waters of the Atlantic. He was forced to lower the plane in search of warmer air. Six pilots had already died attempting to cross the Atlantic. Lindbergh did not want to join them.

But Lindbergh decided not to give up. He believed in the limitless possibilities aviation offered to humankind. With skill and determination, he could accomplish the impossible. Several hours later, the plane had thawed, and he was safe.

Charles Lindbergh stands beside the Spirit of St. Louis.

Lindbergh flew the amazing 33.5 hours from New York to Paris, France. He was the first aviator to do so and was welcomed into the arms of the world as a hero. His victory opened the doors for commercial flight. It also brought new opportunities, and challenges, into Lindbergh's life. He would soon experience both triumph and grief.

ON THE MOVE

Charles Augustus Lindbergh was born in Detroit, Michigan, on February 4, 1902. His parents were Evangeline Lodge Land and Charles Augustus Lindbergh Sr., often called C.A. Charles grew up on a 110-acre (45-ha) farm on the banks of the Mississippi River near Little Falls, Minnesota. C.A. had two daughters from a previous marriage. The daughters' names were Lillian and Eva. But Charles's half sisters were much older than him. He spent most of his time alone or playing with the family dogs.

In 1906, C.A. was elected to the U.S. House of Representatives. The family moved to Washington DC. During the day, Charles went to school. After school, he often visited his father at work. Charles spent hours seated with his father on the floor of the House of Representatives.

Each summer, Charles and his mother took a train to the farm in Little Falls. Along the way, they spent several weeks at Evangeline's home in Detroit. There, Charles visited his grandfather Dr. Charles H. Land.

Land was a dentist and an inventor. His house served as his invention laboratory and office. Land patiently answered all of Charles's questions and let him try out many of his tools.

Charles also showed incredible mechanical ability. He invented a clever system for moving large blocks of ice that had been cut

Young Charles stands beside his father,
Charles Augustus Lindbergh Sr.

from the Mississippi River. The ice blocks were used in an icebox to keep foods cold, much like a modern refrigerator. Charles created a system using wooden planks, rope, a cart, a pulley, and tongs to move the blocks.

Charles also took an early interest in piloting. When he was ten years old, his mother took him to an air show outside Washington DC. He watched an airplane race an automobile. Another plane dropped oranges onto the outline of a battleship. Lindbergh was fascinated by the performance. He thought someday he, too, would like to fly.

In 1920, Lindbergh decided to study engineering at the University of Wisconsin. But he wasn't interested in his courses and didn't study. He did not do well, and at one point was in danger of being expelled.

At college, Lindbergh made few friends. His closest friends were both motorcycle riders. Lindbergh also had a motorcycle, which he had bought in his last year of high school. One of his friends showed Lindbergh some brochures from flying schools. At this time, flying was considered a reckless activity. In fact, insurance companies refused to offer life insurance policies to barnstormers. These flyers toured the country, charging $5 or $10 for airplane rides.

But Lindbergh didn't mind the danger. He had made up his mind to become a pilot. As a child, he had daydreamed about flying. He later wrote, "I spent hours lying on my back . . . staring into the sky. . . . How wonderful would it be, I'd thought, if I had an airplane—wings with which I could fly up to the clouds and explore their caves and canyons—wings like that hawk circling above me."

Lindbergh wrote to an aircraft company in Lincoln, Nebraska. This company offered to give him flying lessons for $500. He decided to drop out of the University of Wisconsin in the middle of his second year. In late March 1922, Lindbergh got on his motorcycle and headed for Lincoln.

Barnstormers perform in the air.

American Moments

THE EAGLE GETS HIS WINGS

Lindbergh arrived at Ray Page's Flying School on April 1. During his first week, he followed the mechanics around the hangar. Lindbergh quickly learned how to service a 150-horsepower engine.

On April 9, 1922, Lindbergh prepared for his first flight in an airplane. He was a passenger. As Lindbergh lifted off the ground, the engine made a deafening roar. He rose up over the treetops and across a ravine. Lindbergh felt like a hawk soaring high over the world below. "Trees become bushes; barns toys; cows turn into rabbits as we climb," he later remembered.

The excitement of his first flight left Lindbergh eager for more. However, the flying school did not work out as he had hoped. The school's only instructor, Ray Page, did not like flying. He often cancelled Lindbergh's lessons. Lindbergh soon learned that Page was going to sell the school's only dual control plane to a barnstormer named Erold Bahl. He decided it was time to find another flying opportunity.

Lindbergh admired Bahl and wanted to be his assistant while barnstorming around Nebraska, Kansas, and Colorado. Bahl agreed to take Lindbergh along. Lindbergh had a daring idea of how to attract spectators. As Bahl flew over a town, Lindbergh stood on the wing and waved to the people below.

10

*A barnstorming performer lowers himself
onto the wing of another plane midair.*

After barnstorming with Bahl, Lindbergh learned how to parachute. At this time, parachutes were new. He then joined a barnstorming tour with Harold J. "Shorty" Lynch. The barnstorming act highlighted Lindbergh as a wing-walker and parachute jumper. Flyers advertised Lynch's star performer, Daredevil Lindbergh.

Lindbergh and Lynch toured for four months in Colorado, Wyoming, Kansas, and Montana. During this time, Lindbergh learned many new stunts. He dangled underneath the plane from a leather strap he held between his teeth. He dazzled crowds by standing on a wing while the plane flew loops.

Lindbergh did not actually hold himself by his teeth. He was suspended by a cable attached to a shoulder harness under his coat. The cable was too thin to be seen by the people below. Lindbergh was able to stand on the wing upside down with the help of four cables and steel foot cups that anchored him to the wing.

Barnstorming stunts kept Lindbergh close to airplanes. But he really wanted to be a pilot. By April 1923, he had enough money to make a down payment on his own plane. *Jenny* was a surplus World War I Curtis JN-4D plane. In his first attempts, he banged up the plane a bit, but eventually he learned to fly it.

Through flight practice, Lindbergh learned how to judge field and weather conditions. He gained experience in making the life-and-death decisions that are essential in a good pilot. Finally, he was ready to barnstorm on his own. His mother even agreed to barnstorm with him. Evangeline threw flyers over the side of the cockpit to the crowds below.

During the summer of 1923, Lindbergh heard of newer, more powerful planes. The only place he would get a chance to fly these newer planes was in the U.S. Army. On March 15, 1924, Lindbergh enrolled as a cadet in the Army Air Service Cadet Program.

After Lindbergh graduated first in his class from training school, he moved to St. Louis, Missouri. He worked as a flight instructor at St. Louis's Lambert Field. Lindbergh became known as one of the best aviators in the country. Not only did Lindbergh have excellent vision and coordination, but he also had good concentration. When faced with danger, he was calm and unshakable.

His skills landed him a job as chief pilot of the St. Louis-Chicago airmail route. Airmail service began in the United States in 1918.

However, the service was dangerous for pilots. The planes were poorly designed and lacked radio communication. Pilots nicknamed the planes "flaming coffins" because the fuel tanks often exploded during landings. Equipment failed in cold temperatures, causing deadly crashes. At the time, flying for the mail service was the most dangerous job in the United States.

The dangers were not enough to keep Lindbergh away. He later commented, "I had been attracted to aviation by its adventure, not its safety." Lindbergh flew his first airmail flight from Chicago, Illinois, to St. Louis, Missouri, on April 26, 1926. He and two other pilots made five round trips a week. Lindbergh's crew set a record for reliability.

Lindbergh and a passenger sit in the Jenny.

FROM NEW YORK TO PARIS

In the fall of 1926, Lindbergh sat in a movie theater, watching newsreels on the screen. The report highlighted French aviator Paul-René Fonck, who was preparing for a nonstop flight across the Atlantic Ocean. Some of the world's best pilots were eager to compete for the $25,000 Orteig prize. This prize would be awarded to the aviator who successfully completed the first transatlantic flight.

Lindbergh considered the flight. He believed planes had advanced to a point where such a flight was possible. More importantly, he believed he could do it. During the past four years, Lindbergh had flown almost 2,000 hours. He often flew at night, through storms, and in cold temperatures. Lindbergh's expert flying skills had earned him a reputation as an incredible pilot.

In order to make the trip, Lindbergh needed a plane and a plan. He talked to several St. Louis businessmen. Lindbergh's key supporter was Harry Knight, president of the St. Louis Flying Club.

The two men met with the head of the St. Louis Chamber of Commerce, Harold Bixby. Lindbergh reminded Bixby that St. Louis already had one of the best commercial airports in the country. If Bixby sponsored a historic transatlantic flight, St. Louis would most

Paul-René Fonck

likely become the leader of commercial aviation. Bixby agreed. A fund of $15,000 was set up.

Lindbergh already had an idea of what kind of plane he should fly. He believed a single-engine plane flown by a lone pilot had the best chance for success. Some supporters disagreed. They thought the plane should have both a pilot and a navigator. The long flight would put too much stress on one pilot. They believed flying solo across the Atlantic Ocean was suicide.

Some experts also argued that the plane should have multiple engines. Lindbergh believed that more than one engine would increase his chances of failure. For one thing, extra engines would make the plane too heavy. It would already be overloaded with fuel. Also, he maintained if one engine failed, the plane would likely not make it back with the other engines.

In the end, Lindbergh won his argument. In February 1927, he contracted Ryan Airlines Corporation of San Diego, California, to build a plane for $6,000. Crews immediately went to work building the *Spirit of St. Louis*.

With only a few weeks to go, Lindbergh worried one of his competitors might beat him. But the other pilots had troubles that caused delays. Fonck damaged his plane in an attempt. A different crew of two pilots lifted off, but never made it to their destination.

These failures did not slow Lindbergh. On May 10, he took off from San Diego in the *Spirit of St. Louis*. He landed at Curtiss Field in Long Island, New York, on May 12. He broke the record for the fastest transcontinental flight.

This flight, and news of the flight he was about to attempt, made Lindbergh famous. Newspapers portrayed him as all-American hero.

Lindbergh works on the engine
of the Spirit of St. Louis.

Headlines dubbed him "The Lone Eagle," "The Flyin' Kid," and "Lucky Lindy." Lindbergh did not appreciate the nicknames. He believed that flying well was a result of hard work, not luck.

On the morning of May 20, Lindbergh arrived at Roosevelt Field in New York City. Weather conditions posed problems for liftoff. Rain had made the field muddy and the winds had shifted. Instead of a helpful tailwind, Lindbergh would have to fight against a headwind.

Lindbergh climbed in the cockpit of the *Spirit of St. Louis*. He fastened his flight helmet and lowered his goggles. He waved to the mechanic to start the propellers. The *Spirit of St. Louis* taxied down the runway. At 7:52 AM Eastern Standard Time, the small plane lifted off for Paris, France.

In the air, Lindbergh established a routine. Every hour, he switched to another fuel tank and marked it in pencil on the upper right side of his instrument panel. Next, he adjusted his magnetic compass to account for changes in Earth's magnetic field.

Although he had sandwiches and a one-quart canteen filled with water, Lindbergh ate and drank very little. He knew the hunger pangs would help keep him awake later in the flight. After several hours, his muscles began to cramp from riding in the tiny cockpit. But the cramp eventually loosened as his body became used to his position.

After nine hours, Lindbergh became overwhelmed with the urge to sleep. He knew fatigue would be his greatest enemy. From time to time, he drifted off to sleep. A wing would dip and awaken him. As night fell, Lindbergh was surrounded by darkness. The only light came from the glow of the instrument dials and his flashlight. Lindbergh relied solely on his instruments to keep him on the right flight path.

At 15 hours, Lindbergh had a scare. Two of his compasses suddenly failed, and his magnetic compass started to swing wildly back and forth. He had heard tales of pilots losing their instruments in magnetic storms. Before long, the compasses began working again. But Lindbergh feared he had flown off course. He used the position of the moon to reestablish his route.

Halfway through the flight, Lindbergh's eyelids became heavy. He desperately fought the urge to sleep. Only the fear of death kept him awake. He repeated to himself, "There's no alternative but death and failure. No alternative but death and failure."

Daybreak finally came 24 hours after liftoff from Roosevelt Field. Lindbergh had survived the night. He descended to 1,500 feet (457 m) and kept a steady speed of 100 miles per hour (161 km/h). After 27 hours, he saw a seagull and knew that land must be near. Shortly after, he spotted a fishing boat in the waters below. Lindbergh tried

The Spirit of St. Louis *in flight*

Paris police form a protective barrier around the Spirit of St. Louis.

shouting to the boat, asking for directions to Ireland. But the men onboard could not hear him over the rumble of his engine.

However, Lindbergh did not need to worry. Despite fatigue, flying by instruments, and unknown crosswinds, he was still on course. Lindbergh's remarkable piloting had brought him across the Atlantic two and a half hours ahead of schedule. And now he was wide awake at last.

On May 21, 1927, the *Spirit of St. Louis* flew into Le Bourget Airport in Paris at 10:22 PM Paris time. A crowd of 100,000 people showed up to give Lindbergh a hero's welcome. After 33.5 hours in flight, Lindbergh was pulled from the cockpit by the crowd. People pushed and shoved, hoping to get a glimpse of the brave young pilot.

Lindbergh knew his life was about to change. "I had entered a new environment of life and found myself surrounded by unforeseen opportunities, responsibilities, and problems," he said.

Lindbergh flies over
Paris, France.

THE AMERICAN HERO

After landing in Paris, Lindbergh flew to Brussels, Belgium, and London, England. At each stop, his heroic feat was celebrated with public ceremonies. Overnight, Lindbergh had become famous. The entire world wanted to hear how a Minnesota farm boy had beaten the world's greatest aviators.

U.S. president Calvin Coolidge sent the cruiser USS *Memphis* to London to bring Lindbergh and the *Spirit of St. Louis* back home. Americans welcomed their hero with huge parades in Washington DC and New York City. Coolidge awarded Lindbergh the Distinguished Flying Cross and the Congressional Medal of Honor.

Lindbergh's daily life was forever changed. Crowds of people followed him wherever he went. Reporters and photographers hounded him day and night. He could no longer go to a movie or take a walk without being recognized.

He decided to use his fame to promote aviation. In July 1927, Lindbergh began a tour across the United States in the *Spirit of St. Louis*. He stressed safety and being on time. He wanted to show Americans that air travel was dependable.

The tour ended in late October. Lindbergh had covered 22,340 miles (35,953 km) and had flown 260 hours. Over four months, he

Calvin Coolidge

gave 147 speeches and rode 1,285 miles (2,068 km) in parades. His visits brought $100 million in new aviation construction.

Two months later, Lindbergh attempted another nonstop flight. This time, he took off from Washington DC and flew to Mexico City, Mexico. Dwight Morrow, the U.S. ambassador to Mexico, suggested the trip. For years, poor relations existed between the United States and Mexico. Morrow hoped a visit from the world-famous pilot would improve relations.

However, Lindbergh's 2,100-mile (3,380-km) flight to Mexico was dangerous. He flew through heavy rains and thick fog. At one point he even flew off course. By noon, crowds in Mexico City stood with their heads tilted to the sky. The typically on-time aviator was late.

Morrow began to worry that something tragic had happened. But at 2:40 PM, Lindbergh touched down in Mexico City. The American hero came through after 27.5 hours in the air.

Now at age 25, Lindbergh had begun thinking about marriage. He wanted to marry someone who would learn to fly. Lindbergh met Ambassador Morrow's 21-year-old daughter, Anne. He visited her at the Morrows' estate in Englewood, New Jersey. Lindbergh took her flying and for drives through the New Jersey countryside.

Before long, Lindbergh knew he wanted to marry her. On May 27, 1929, Charles and Anne were married at Englewood. Lindbergh taught Anne how to pilot a plane. She soon became his navigator. Anne also learned to operate a radio and send Morse code.

The press continued to pester the Lindberghs. Newspaper reporters paid airport workers for any information they could offer about the famous flyer. Charles and Anne were followed wherever they went. He began to despise the media.

Charles Lindbergh Jr. sits between Bogey and Skean.

But Lindbergh did have reasons to be happy. On June 22, 1930, Anne gave birth to Charles Augustus Lindbergh Jr. The baby was born at their apartment in New York City. Anne was afraid she would not have any privacy at the hospital.

Lindbergh served as a technical advisor for Transcontinental Air Transport and Pan American World Airways, Inc. He mapped new air routes and helped decide what planes to buy and where to build airport terminals. He also worked to establish the first transcontinental airline service.

Lindbergh's work for the air services brought an exciting opportunity. At the end of July 1931, Charles and Anne set out on a journey over the Arctic to East Asia. Over the next several months, the couple surveyed possible air routes between the United States and China. Charles Jr., or Charlie, stayed with Anne's parents while they were gone.

After returning home, the Lindberghs decided to build a house. They bought a 400-acre (162-ha) lot in Hopewell, New Jersey. Woods screened the property. This, unfortunately, did not keep the press away. When the house was nearly finished, the Lindberghs began spending weekends there. During the week, they would return to the Morrows' Englewood estate.

The last week in February 1932, Charlie caught a cold. Instead of returning to Englewood, the couple decided to stay in Hopewell. Anne called Englewood and asked the baby's nurse to come help take care of the sick child. On March 1, Anne and the nurse, Betty Gow, got Charlie ready for bed.

At 7:30 PM, Anne and Gow closed and bolted all the shutters, except at one window. At this window, a shutter was warped and would not close all the way. Anne then went downstairs. Gow began cleaning in other rooms. The nurse checked on Charlie around 8:00 PM. He was fast asleep in his crib. At 10:00 PM, Gow went into Charlie's room again. The baby was gone.

The Lindberghs called the police. When police arrived, they found footprints leading away from the house. It looked like the kidnapper wore burlap sacks over his or her shoes to cover any shoe prints. A ladder was leaning against the house next to the window with the broken shutter.

A ransom note was found on the windowsill. It asked for $50,000. The note suggested that there was more than one kidnapper. It also stated that they would contact Lindbergh and let him know where to deliver the money. The kidnappers promised the baby was in good care. They also instructed him not to tell the police.

26

WANTED

INFORMATION AS TO THE WHEREABOUTS OF

CHAS. A. LINDBERGH, Jr.

OF HOPEWELL, N. J.

SON OF COL. CHAS. A. LINDBERGH

World-Famous Aviator

This child was kidnaped from his home in Hopewell, N. J., between 8 and 10 p. m. on Tuesday, March 1, 1932.

DESCRIPTION:

Age, 20 months   Hair, blond, curly
Weight, 27 to 30 lbs.   Eyes, dark blue
Height, 29 inches   Complexion, light

Deep dimple in center of chin
Dressed in one-piece coverall night suit

ADDRESS ALL COMMUNICATIONS TO
COL. H. N. SCHWARZKOPF, TRENTON, N. J., or
COL. CHAS. A. LINDBERGH, HOPEWELL, N. J.

ALL COMMUNICATIONS WILL BE TREATED IN CONFIDENCE

March 11, 1932

COL. H. NORMAN SCHWARZKOPF
Supt. New Jersey State Police, Trenton, N. J.

This poster asks for information about the Lindbergh kidnapping. The U.S. Department of Justice distributed this poster in more than 1,400 cities.

But it was too late to keep the kidnapping a secret. By 10:30 PM, news bulletins about the kidnapping interrupted radio programs. The next morning, the story headlined newspapers across the country. The kidnapping sparked a nationwide manhunt. Police stopped any parents with a child who looked about the same age as Charlie. At the Lindbergh's home, reporters and the public swarmed the house. The crowds trampled any possible evidence on the lawn.

The ransom was soon raised to $70,000. One week after the kidnapping, a 72-year-old retired teacher phoned Lindbergh. The caller, John F. Condon, offered to help Lindbergh. Lindbergh accepted his offer. Condon met several times with one of the supposed kidnappers. They met in a cemetery so the kidnapper got the name Graveyard John. The baby was never along. Condon refused to give Graveyard John the ransom money unless he handed the baby over. Graveyard John refused to give up Charlie, but insisted the child was alive and well.

On April 2, Condon had a final meeting with Graveyard John. Again, Charlie was not there. Reluctantly, Condon handed over the money, and Graveyard John gave him a note. The note said that Charlie was on a boat named the *Nelly*. The baby was supposedly there with two innocent people. But there was no *Nelly*, and no baby.

The search for little Charlie ended on May 12. A truck driver found the body of what appeared to be a baby near the Lindbergh's home. Examination showed the baby had died two to three months earlier. Lindbergh identified the body as his son's. It is believed that Charlie was killed the night of the kidnapping.

John F. Condon

Lindbergh continued to devote all of his time to the investigation. The ransom bills had been marked. The police hoped the kidnappers would start spending the money so authorities could trace it.

Months later, a trace was made. Police arrested Bruno Richard Hauptmann and searched his house. The house was near the cemetery where Condon had met with Graveyard John. They found some of the ransom money hidden in his garage. Police also found road maps of New Jersey, binoculars, and a notebook drawing of a ladder and two windows.

A jury found Hauptmann guilty of Charlie's murder. On the evening of April 3, 1936, Hauptmann was strapped into an electric chair at New Jersey State prison. Three minutes later, he was dead.

The Lindberghs tried to go on with their lives. On August 6, 1932, the second of their six children, Jon, was born. Shortly after his birth, the couple received hundreds of letters threatening to kidnap the boy. The family left Hopewell for good and moved into the Englewood estate.

State troopers constantly patrolled the area, and Lindbergh bought Thor, a German shepherd guard dog. But Lindbergh came to believe that the public would never leave his family alone. He decided the only way to keep his family safe was to move out of the country.

The Englewood estate

HAUPTMANN TRIAL CONTROVERSY

Bruno Richard Hauptmann in jail

At the time of Bruno Richard Hauptmann's conviction, few questioned his guilt. The United States was having problems with Germany, and Hauptmann was a German immigrant. This, unfortunately, inspired prejudiced feelings against him. However, in the years after the trial, many questions about Hauptmann's guilt have been raised.

One troubling issue is that Hauptmann's lawyer, Edward Reilly, was hired by the Hearst organization. The Hearst organization printed newspapers and was known to believe that Hauptmann was guilty. Reilly did a very poor job of defending Hauptmann. Some have wondered if Reilly did so on purpose.

Many also now believe that evidence in the case was tampered with by reporters and police. Several witnesses in the case have also come to be considered unreliable. One man who claimed to have seen Hauptmann was partially blind in both eyes. This same man later identified a cabinet as a woman wearing a hat. Despite the questions, the ruling in Hauptmann's case has never been reversed.

FLEEING AMERICA

On December 22, 1935, Lindbergh, Anne, and Jon boarded a freighter ship for Liverpool, England. The American public did not know of their departure. The ship's crew did not even know the Lindberghs were aboard until after they had set sail.

The Lindberghs found a house in the English countryside near London. At first, English reporters were no better than the Americans. But interest in the Lindberghs faded. Charles and Anne finally began to enjoy the privacy they had so long hoped for.

Late in the spring of 1936, Lindbergh received a request from Truman Smith, the military attaché to the U.S. embassy in Berlin, Germany. Hermann Göring, the head of German aviation, had invited Lindbergh to visit Germany. Göring wanted him to see the great progress the Germans were making in flight.

After Germany's defeat in World War I, the German military was disarmed. But in 1933, Adolf Hitler and the Nazi Party came to power in Germany. The country again started to build up its military. The United States did not know the power of the German air force, the Luftwaffe. Any information Lindbergh could learn would be useful for U.S. intelligence.

For this reason, Charles and Anne agreed to go. Lindbergh toured the military flying fields, research laboratories, and aircraft factories.

Hermann Göring (right) shows a ceremonial sword to Lindbergh.

He was impressed with the strength of the Luftwaffe. Lindbergh also seemed to admire Hitler's vision for a greater country.

When he returned to England, Lindbergh reported to English officials. He stressed the strength of the Luftwaffe and urged England to take action. He thought they should rapidly build up their own air fleet. But officials did not take action right away.

Lindbergh was frustrated that he made the trip for nothing. He and Anne went back to their lives. In the spring of 1937, Anne gave birth in London to a third son, Land. He was named after Lindbergh's grandfather Land.

That fall, Lindbergh received a second invitation to Germany. He was asked to attend an aviation congress in Munich. At the congress, Lindbergh met Ernst Udet, a World War I German flying ace. Udet took Lindbergh to a top-secret military airfield. Lindbergh inspected seven of the latest German warplanes. He even flew a new bomber.

After his visit to the airfield, Lindbergh wrote a report for the U.S. military. He emphasized the strength of the German air force. But the report did not mention any weaknesses. The Luftwaffe lacked long-range bombers and had few experienced officers. Some U.S. officials questioned Lindbergh's loyalty to the United States.

In 1938, Lindbergh moved his family to Illiec, a remote island off the coast of France. He bought a home near French scientist Dr. Alexis Carrel. Lindbergh and Carrel had worked together years before to create a perfusion pump for heart surgery. They had also cowritten a book called *The Culture of Organs*. Under Carrel's influence, Lindbergh began researching how to extend the human lifespan. He even set up a laboratory in his house.

Ernst Udet

Carrel had many radical ideas. He thought whites were a superior race. He also believed criminals and mentally ill people should be exterminated. Lindbergh agreed with many of Carrel's ideas.

Charles and Anne flew to Berlin for another aviation conference in October 1938. The couple even considered moving to Berlin with their children. Lindbergh liked the way the press never bothered him in Germany.

On October 19, Lindbergh was the guest of honor at a dinner in Berlin. There, Göring presented Lindbergh with the Service Cross of the German Eagle. This award is the second highest of all German decorations. Lindbergh wore the medal all evening.

Dr. Alexis Carrel

Anne worried about the award. She thought it might cause trouble for her husband. But Lindbergh ignored her concerns. As it turned out, Anne was right. News of the award in England, France, and the United States brought reactions ranging from shock to anger. With all these countries on the verge of war, it seemed un-American for Lindbergh to accept such a medal.

Men pass shattered windows after the violence of Kristallnacht.

On November 9, the Nazis attacked Jewish businesses and synagogues throughout Germany and Austria. Store windows were smashed and more than 1,000 synagogues were set on fire or damaged. So much glass littered the streets that the attack became known as *Kristallnacht* or "night of broken glass."

More than 100 Jewish people were killed on *Kristallnacht*. Thousands more were arrested trying to defend their businesses. Lindbergh made no public comment on the assault, but decided not to spend his winter in Germany.

In the spring of 1939, General Henry H. Arnold, chief of the U.S. Army Air Corps, asked Lindbergh to return to the United States. Lindbergh was a colonel in the U.S. Air Corps Reserve. General Arnold wanted his advice on how to strengthen the United States's air force. So on April 14, Lindbergh sailed to the United States.

HATRED AND HEROISM

Upon his arrival, Lindbergh was immediately swamped with meetings. It was decided that a huge buildup of the Army Air Corps was needed. Congress spent millions of dollars for the cause, with a goal of building 6,000 new warplanes.

Through the spring and summer, Lindbergh toured the United States. He inspected aircraft research facilities and manufacturing plants across the country. Lindbergh performed his service to the Army, but he did not support war. He believed France and England were too weak to defend themselves. He also thought the United States should stay out of the war. This theory is called isolationism.

On September 1, 1939, Germany invaded Poland, sparking World War II. France and England, which had an alliance with Poland, declared war on Germany. This did not, however, cause Lindbergh to change his mind about the war. He still advocated that the United States stay out of it.

Lindbergh soon asked to be released from active duty. His request was granted on September 14, 1939. Lindbergh decided to join the America First Committee and speak out against American involvement in the war. His speeches brought both support and criticism.

As the war in Europe raged on, Lindbergh continued to support isolationism in speeches. He also advocated white supremacy and

*Lindbergh enrolls in the America First Committee.
Seated to his left is R. Douglas Stuart Jr.*

expressed ideas bordering on anti-Semitic. One such questionable speech occurred on September 11, 1941, in Des Moines, Iowa. There, he said, "Instead of agitating for war, Jews in this country should be opposing it in every way. . . . Their greatest danger to this country lies in their large ownership and influence in our motion pictures, our press, our radio and our government."

Many Americans thought Lindbergh was pro-Nazi. Eventually, even his supporters began to question his loyalty. The great American hero was slowly losing his spotless reputation.

Despite all of Lindbergh's protests, the United States entered World War II in December 1941. On December 7, Japan attacked Pearl Harbor, Hawaii. Congress declared war shortly afterward.

Lindbergh was eager to join the war effort. President Franklin D. Roosevelt, however, would not allow it. Lindbergh had spoken out against the Roosevelt administration and the war. "You can't

have an officer leading men who thinks we're licked before we start
. . . " Roosevelt said.

Despite Roosevelt's discouragement, Lindbergh did help the
United States during the war. He worked with Henry Ford to build
B-24 bombers. In 1943, United Aircraft sent Lindbergh to the
Pacific. He was supposed to be an observer. But Lindbergh ended up
flying more than 50 combat missions.

After the war, Lindbergh served as a consultant for many
organizations. These included Pan American World Airways, the
U.S. Department of Defense, and the National Advisory Committee
for Aeronautics (NACA). In 1953, Lindbergh's book *The Spirit of St.
Louis* won a Pulitzer Prize. The following year, President Dwight D.
Eisenhower made him a brigadier general in the Air Force Reserve.

When Lindbergh flew, he began to notice changes taking place all
over the world. Thick forests were being chopped down. Towns rose
up out of open prairie land. In the mid-1960s, Lindbergh became an
active supporter of the World Wildlife Fund. He also became
involved with organizations such as the International Union for the
Conservation of Nature and the Nature Conservancy. He worked to
create state and national parks. "Where civilization is most advanced,
few birds exist," he wrote. "I realized that if I had to choose, I would
rather have birds than airplanes."

Lindbergh traveled all over the world in an effort to save
endangered species and protect wildlife. In Peru, he asked the
country's president to protect the humpback and blue whales from
whalers. He flew to Alaska to urge the state legislature to stop
paying hunters to kill wolves. Wherever he went, his fame as a pilot
caught people's attention. And they listened to what he had to say.

Lindbergh stands to the left of the Spirit of St. Louis.

In 1972, Lindbergh was diagnosed with cancer of the lymph nodes. After battling the disease for a little more than a year, Lindbergh learned he only had a few months to live. He spent the last days of his life at a quiet cottage on Maui in the Hawaiian Islands. On August 26, 1974, he died at the age of 72 with his wife, Anne, and son Land at his side. Today, the world still marvels at the life of this legendary hero.

TIMELINE

1902   On February 4, Charles Augustus Lindbergh is born in Detroit, Michigan.

1922   In March, Lindbergh enrolls in flight school in Lincoln, Nebraska.

1924   Lindbergh enrolls as a cadet in the Army Air Service Cadet Program.

1926   Lindbergh decides to compete for the $25,000 Orteig prize by flying across the Atlantic Ocean. He soon gets financial backing for this goal.

1927   In February, Lindbergh contracts Ryan Airlines Corporation in San Diego, California, to build the *Spirit of St. Louis*.

On May 12, Lindbergh breaks the record for fastest transcontinental flight. He flew from San Diego, California, to Long Island, New York.

On May 20, Lindbergh takes off from New York City, New York, and begins the world's first transatlantic flight.

On May 21, Lindbergh lands in Paris, France, after 33.5 hours in the air.

From July to October, Lindbergh tours the United States in the *Spirit of St. Louis* to promote aviation.

1929 Lindbergh marries Anne Marrow. The next year, their son, Charlie, is born.

1932 On March 1, Lindbergh's son, Charlie, is kidnapped.

On May 12, Charlie's body is discovered. Bruno Richard Hauptmann is later found guilty of the baby's murder and executed.

1935 The Lindberghs move to England.

1939 to 1945 World War II is fought. It begins when Germany invades Poland on September 1, 1939. The United States enters the war in December 1941 after Japan bombs Pearl Harbor, Hawaii.

1953 Lindbergh wins a Pulitzer Prize for his book *The Spirit of St. Louis*.

1974 On August 26, Lindbergh dies of cancer.

American Moments

FAST FACTS

Charles H. Land was the first doctor to use porcelain in dental crowns. Among his many inventions was a self-bouncing cradle, which Charles Lindbergh used as a baby. Land also developed an air-filtering system because he believed the recently invented automobiles were polluting the air.

Lindbergh was awarded the first Distinguished Flying Cross ever. Since then, other recipients have included former president George H.W. Bush and astronaut Virgil "Gus" Grissom.

As a result of the kidnapping of Charlie Lindbergh, the U.S. Congress passed the Lindbergh Act. This act made kidnapping a federal crime. It also allowed federal officers to pursue kidnappers across state borders.

Before her death on February 7, 2001, Anne Morrow Lindbergh had written 11 books. Her most popular book, *Gift from the Sea*, has sold more than 1 million copies.

To mark the seventy-fifth anniversary of his grandfather's transatlantic flight, Eric Lindbergh repeated Charles Lindbergh's journey. On May 2, 2002, Eric landed in Paris, France, after taking off from New York 17 hours and 7 minutes earlier.

WEB SITES
WWW.ABDOPUB.COM

Would you like to learn more about the *Spirit of St. Louis*? Please visit **www.abdopub.com** to find up-to-date Web site links about the *Spirit of St. Louis* and other American moments. These links are routinely monitored and updated to provide the most current information available.

Lindbergh seated inside the Spirit of St. Louis

GLOSSARY

America First Committee: an influential political group that existed between 1940 and 1941. The committee opposed U.S. involvement in World War II until the bombing of Pearl Harbor, Hawaii, on December 7, 1941. Afterward, the committee dissolved and encouraged its members to support the war.

anti-Semitism: discrimination against Jewish people.

barnstorm: to travel around the countryside in an airplane, offering rides and performing stunts.

congress: a formal meeting of delegates for discussion and usually action on some question.

isolationism: a policy in which a country does not participate in economic or political relations with other countries.

lymph nodes: glands located in the neck, armpit, and groin that filter bacteria and other harmful particles out of the body.

magnetic storm: a disturbance in Earth's magnetic field caused by solar flares.

Morse code: a code invented by Samuel A. Morse in which letters and numbers are represented by a series of long and short signals called dots and dashes. This code was first used over the telegraph in an audio fashion. It can also be transmitted visually.

newsreel: a short movie that relates current events.

perfusion pump: a device that keeps blood circulating during heart surgery.

ransom: money demanded in return for the release of someone or something in captivity.

synagogue: a Jewish place of worship.

transatlantic: crossing the Atlantic Ocean.

transcontinental: crossing a continent.

whaling: an industry in which whales are hunted for the commercial use of their oil, bones, and other parts. People who participate in this industry are known as whalers.

white supremacy: a belief in the superiority of the white race over other races. White supremacy holds that whites should be dominant over all other groups. People who hold this belief are called white supremacists.

World War I: 1914 to 1918, fought in Europe. The United States, Great Britain, France, Russia, and their allies were on one side. Germany, Austria-Hungary, and their allies were on the other side. The war began when Archduke Ferdinand of Austria was assassinated. The United States joined the war in 1917 because Germany began attacking ships that weren't involved in the war.

World War II: 1939 to 1945, fought in Europe, Asia, and Africa. The United States, France, Great Britain, the Soviet Union, and their allies were on one side. Germany, Italy, Japan, and their allies were on the other side. The war began when Germany invaded Poland. The United States entered the war in 1941 after Japan bombed Pearl Harbor, Hawaii.

INDEX